SPORTS BRANDS

PATAGONIA

BY ALEXIS BURLING

Content Consultant
Huiju Park, PhD
Associate Professor of Apparel Design
College of Human Ecology
Cornell University

Essential Library
An Imprint of Abdo Publishing
abdobooks.com

ABDOBOOKS.COM

Published by Abdo Publishing, a division of ABDO, PO Box 398166, Minneapolis, Minnesota 55439. Copyright © 2023 by Abdo Consulting Group, Inc. International copyrights reserved in all countries. No part of this book may be reproduced in any form without written permission from the publisher. Essential Library™ is a trademark and logo of Abdo Publishing.

Printed in the United States of America, North Mankato, Minnesota.
052022
092022

Cover Photo: Sergio Pitamitz/Danita Delimont/Danita Delimont Photography/Newscom
Interior Photos: Shutterstock Images, 4–5, 42, 43, 97; Moreno Soppelsa/Shutterstock Images, 8; Egoreichenkov Evgenii/Shutterstock Images, 13; Tada Images/Shutterstock Images, 15; Jean-Marc Giboux/Hulton Archive/Getty Images, 16–17; Denver Post/Getty Images, 19; Jonathan Alcorn/ZUMA Press, Inc./Alamy, 23; Greg Epperson/Shutterstock Images, 25; Robert Landau/Alamy, 28–29; Roman Tiraspolsky/Shutterstock Images, 32; Cecile Marion/Alamy, 37; Al Seib/Los Angeles Times/Getty Images, 38–39; Amanda Whitlock/The Southern/AP Images, 44; Tobias Hase/Picture Alliance/DPA/AP Images, 49; David Walter Banks/The Washington Post/Getty Images, 50–51, 55, 58, 62–63; Bethany Mollenkof/Los Angeles Times/Getty Images, 68–69; Terry Straehley/Shutterstock Images, 72; Ivan River/Shutterstock Images, 74–75; T. Hoffman/Shutterstock Images, 80–81; J. Daracunas/Shutterstock Images, 82; Mandel Ngan/AFP/Getty Images, 86; Budrul Chukrut/SOPA Images/Sipa USA/AP Images, 88–89; Editorial Image, LLC/Alamy, 92–93; Ben Gabbe/Tribeca X/Getty Images Entertainment/Getty Images, 98

Editor: Arnold Ringstad
Series Designer: Sarah Taplin

Library of Congress Control Number: 2021951568
Publisher's Cataloging-in-Publication Data
Names: Burling, Alexis, author.
Title: Patagonia / by Alexis Burling.
Description: Minneapolis, Minnesota : Abdo Publishing, 2023 | Series: Sports brands | Includes online resources and index.
Identifiers: ISBN 9781532198144 (lib. bdg.) | ISBN 9781098271794 (ebook)
Subjects: LCSH: Clothing and dress--Juvenile literature. | Patagonia, Inc.--Juvenile literature. | Sport clothes industry--Juvenile literature. | Brand name products--Juvenile literature.
Classification: DDC 338.7--dc23

CONTENTS

CHAPTER ONE
AN ENVIRONMENTALLY AWARE BRAND 4

CHAPTER TWO
A NATURALIST'S BEGINNING. 16

CHAPTER THREE
THE BIRTH OF PATAGONIA 28

CHAPTER FOUR
A CLOTHING REVOLUTION 38

CHAPTER FIVE
PATAGONIA: AT THE OFFICE. 50

CHAPTER SIX
THE DO-GOOD COMPANY. 62

CHAPTER SEVEN
BRAND CONTROVERSIES 74

CHAPTER EIGHT
"SAVE OUR HOME PLANET". 88

ESSENTIAL FACTS	100	INDEX	110
GLOSSARY	102	ABOUT THE AUTHOR	112
ADDITIONAL RESOURCES	104	ABOUT THE CONSULTANT	112
SOURCE NOTES	106		

CHAPTER ONE

AN ENVIRONMENTALLY AWARE BRAND

Mark Little isn't your average office worker. He commutes on his bike 10 miles (16 km) every day to work. He also loves his job. Little works for world-renowned Patagonia, overseeing the outdoor brand's lines of men's sportswear and surf products. Much of his wardrobe is made up of Patagonia's vast array of cozy wool sweaters, rugged pants and shorts, waterproof rain shells, and insulating puffer jackets.

Though Patagonia is known for its gear for fly-fishing, hiking, camping, rock climbing, and other activities, Little also stands by Patagonia's jeans. In fact, he wore his favorite pair nearly every day for two and a half years after the product team designed them in 2015. "They were my work

> *Patagonia makes a wide variety of clothing designed for outdoor lifestyles.*

uniform, my home uniform, my travel uniform," Little said in an interview with Patagonia's Rachel G. Clark in 2020. "And I think they were washed maybe five times over that span of time."

Clark was flabbergasted, not to mention a little grossed out by that news. When she asked Little why he basically never washed his jeans, he responded matter-of-factly. "Due to the characteristics of our new dye, they started out, well, kind of purplish," Little said. "The team didn't think they could be worn-in and distressed to look like a traditionally dyed pair, so I wanted to prove them wrong."

Little's jeans had that classic worn-in, laid-back look. They included a few hard-earned holes and rips from everyday wear. There were also some stains and faded sections, especially the areas on his thighs where Little wiped his hands after washing them.

THE MARK LITTLE METHOD

According to Mark Little, washing and drying jeans all the time has a big impact on the environment. It takes a lot of energy to fully dry a soaked pair. To minimize environmental impact and prevent fading, Little has five major tips. First, don't wash them often. Instead, spot clean them or place them in the freezer overnight to get rid of smells. Second, wash jeans in cold water and by hand if possible. Third, line dry or dry on low heat. Fourth, repair them before ditching them altogether. Last, when their time is up, donate them to someone else to restart their jean journey.

"I think the knee holes are from me often kneeling when reviewing products at work or horsing around with my pups," he said.

For more than two years, Little wore the jeans around the house and to work. They were also his wardrobe item of choice on hikes in the Dolomites and the John Muir Wilderness; on city strolls through the neighborhoods of London, England; on a flight to Paris, France; and to dinner engagements in Tokyo and Kyoto, Japan. The jeans had literally been around the world and back again. "To me, jeans are like a walking diary. If you choose to truly break them in like I did, they mold to you, become a part of you," Little said.[1]

MAKING ENVIRONMENTALLY RESPONSIBLE JEANS

Patagonia made its first pair of jeans in 1998. But the process of creating them didn't always match the company's environmental values. Though Patagonia was one of the first brands to create jeans using organic cotton, the dyeing process still produced a lot of waste. So, the company scrapped the jeans from its line altogether in order to research a more environmentally friendly dyeing method.

> *Patagonia rethought traditional methods of denim production.*

When companies make jeans using the traditional method, they soak the fabric in big vats. They dump the used dye solution into waterways, with or without treatment, which causes serious pollution. Then they refill the vats to start the process again. "Most jeans (even light- or medium-blue shades) begin their lives as dark jeans. To get them to look worn-in and used, [most companies] wash them in a ton of chemical solutions, stonewash them or intentionally destroy them a little bit,"

STRAIGHT FIT JEANS

PRODUCT SPOTLIGHT

Jeans come in all shapes, sizes, and cuts, but the midweight, five-pocket Straight Fit Jeans from Patagonia are special for one major reason. They're dyed with a unique process that uses less energy and water. When compared with conventional dyeing processes, Patagonia's method also reduces carbon dioxide emissions. For example, the jeans made for women are dyed with an indigo foam instead of huge vats of liquid dye. This helps reduce the carbon impact and water usage significantly.

The women's version comes in one length, with a 27-inch inseam and a high-rise waist that molds to the body's natural shape for a stay-put fit. The men's version comes in regular (32-inch inseam) and short (30-inch inseam). Its denim has some stretch, and it wicks moisture away from the skin. Both the women's and men's jeans are made in Sri Lanka by a Fair Trade Certified factory.

Little said. "The finishing process is the most damaging part of the whole production cycle. Finish-processes may reduce the strength of the fabric by 50 percent or more, resulting in a much lower technical lifetime."[2]

When Patagonia's line of revamped jeans came back on the market in 2015, the dyeing process was better than the traditional method because it required only one reusable vat. It produced fewer carbon emissions and also used less water and less electricity. But there was still a problem: the jeans looked purple and required frequent wear for the color to fade into a more fashionable blue. Wearing the jeans constantly might have worked for Little, but Patagonia was determined to find a better way.

"We knew that if we kept making purple pants, people might not dedicate two and a half years of daily wear to transform them into a desired hue, which meant the jeans might not be worn, loved and kept forever," said Clark. "And we knew that when it came to jeans, one of everyone's closet staples, the key to a truly responsible pair was longevity—they needed to look good enough to wear every day and still be durable enough to keep wearing for a lifetime."[3]

So Little and the rest of the Patagonia team went back to the drawing board. After years of research and product testing, a new type of process emerged. The new indigo-dye solution used waterless foam that sat on top of the fabric rather than being stored in a large soaking vat. It saved energy and water during production. The end result was a lovely dark blue color instead of a garish purple.

Patagonia's design team also upgraded the jeans' material makeup. The new line was made with sustainably grown Regenerative Organic Certified cotton, recycled cotton, and a small amount of spandex for stretch. "Our data for a long time indicated that organic or Regenerative Organic cotton paired with recycled cotton is a winning combination in terms of greenhouse gas emissions and water usage," said Stephanie Karba, environmental researcher at Patagonia. "We thought it was the best way to get energy and water savings and still support farming communities. And that's what we set out to do."[4]

THE ADVANCED DENIM METHOD

The traditional method of coloring jeans with indigo dye is harmful to the environment. So Patagonia researched and came up with a way to streamline the process to make it more environmentally friendly. Advanced Denim technology is a method that uses sulfur-based dyes that bond more easily to fabric than indigo does. The production process is shorter. It also uses 84 percent less water and 30 percent less total energy, and it generates 25 percent fewer carbon emissions.[5] Today, Advanced Denim technology is used by Patagonia and several small brands in Europe.

BUILDING AN ENVIRONMENTALLY CONSCIOUS EMPIRE

Patagonia's search for a way to create the perfect jeans with the least amount of environmental harm is emblematic of how the company approaches creating and selling its outdoor gear. This process is repeatedly refined and updated for the best results possible. "This denim represents as good as we know how to do it at the moment," says Helena Barbour, who leads Patagonia's Life Outdoors business. "And I am an optimist, so I like to think there's even better stuff around the corner."[6]

But perfecting rugged sweaters for everyday wear, long-lasting workwear, and lightweight garments for backpacking, fly-fishing, yoga, and more isn't the only area in which Patagonia excels. The brand is also known for its

IRONCLAD GUARANTEE

Patagonia stands by its products. But it also cares about its customers' satisfaction. Each and every base layer, hoodie, pair of leggings, and sleeping bag is backed by what the brand calls an "ironclad guarantee" for the lifetime of the product. If it doesn't hold up in the way the product was intended during use—for example, if a new pair of hiking pants splits during a multiday mountain trek—it can be returned to the store for a repair, replacement, or refund. Damage due to misuse or regular wear and tear over a long period of time can be repaired for a small fee.

> *Patagonia's gear is designed for outdoor adventures of all kinds.*

environmental stewardship. It has completed hundreds of environmental and social activism campaigns since its founding in 1973, with still more currently underway.

According to its employees, the brand with more than $1 billion in annual revenue is a great place to work too. In November 2021, more than 2,400 people worked at Patagonia, many of whom gave their company culture an "A" rating.[7] The company has offices in the United States, the Netherlands, Japan, South Korea, Australia, Chile, and Argentina. It also operates two distribution centers and runs more than 70 Patagonia stores worldwide.[8]

Perhaps Patagonia's overall appeal can best be summed up by its mission statement. "At Patagonia, we appreciate that all life on earth is under threat of extinction. We aim to use the resources we have—our business, our investments,

PATAGONIA BY THE NUMBERS

Patagonia is known for its awareness and activism on a wide array of issues, from the environmental impact of clothing production to salmon fishing on the Columbia River. In 2020, 100 percent of the company's electricity needs in the United States were met with renewable energy. One hundred percent of the virgin down feathers it uses are certified to the Advanced Global Traceable Down Standard. Ninety-four percent of its products are made with recycled materials. Eighty-five percent of its products are Fair Trade Certified. Patagonia also kept 527 tons (478 metric tons) of plastic out of the world's oceans by turning fishing nets into outdoor gear.[9]

> *Patagonia stores around the world carry forward the brand's unique dedication to social and ecological responsibility.*

our voice and our imaginations—to do something about it," the brand's website states. "Staying true to our core values during forty-plus years in business has helped us create a company we're proud to run and work for. To stay in business for at least forty more, we must defend the place we all call home."[10]

CHAPTER TWO

A NATURALIST'S BEGINNING

Some people who form influential multinational companies start off early with the entrepreneurial spirit. For example, Facebook and Snapchat creators Mark Zuckerberg and Evan Spiegel became millionaires before they even turned 30. But Patagonia founder Yvon Chouinard wasn't planning on starting one of the most popular and eco-conscious clothing brands in the world. In fact, when he was growing up, he wanted to be something totally different. "No young kid growing up ever dreams of someday becoming a businessman," wrote Chouinard in his autobiography, *Let My People Go Surfing: The Education*

> *Patagonia founder Yvon Chouinard had a background in outdoor adventure, not business, when he created the company.*

A RUGGED CHILDHOOD

As a young boy, Yvon Chouinard wasn't a great student. At his parochial school in Burbank, California, he got Ds in many of his classes and had few friends. Instead of studying, he spent most of his free time outside. He fished and hunted for frogs, crawdads, and rabbits. He also tried diving for lobster and abalone off California's Malibu coast. But it was Yvon's membership in his high school's falconry club that changed the course of his life forever. While searching for hawks' nests, he learned to rappel down cliffs. On one of the club's many excursions, he met a fellow outdoors enthusiast who scrambled up rocks rather than down them. Then and there, Yvon's love for rock climbing was born.

of a Reluctant Businessman. "I wanted to be a fur trapper when I grew up."[1]

Yvon was born on November 9, 1938, in Lisbon, Maine, where his mother, Yvonne, grew up. The family spoke only French to each other until Yvon was seven years old. His Québécois father, Gerard, knew his way around both his house and the land. Gerard could fix everything from the plumbing in the bathroom to the cracking plaster on the walls. He was also an electrician and an avid carpenter.

As a boy, Yvon adored fishing and got interested in rock climbing. In 1946, when he and his family moved to Burbank, California, his love for the outdoors grew. He joined the falconry club at his new school. He took up surfing and became obsessed with the West Coast's

> *Climbing was a longtime passion for Chouinard.*

massive waves. He also continued climbing and rappelling down cliffs.

When Yvon was 16, he drove from California to Wyoming in a 1940 Ford he'd rebuilt. He spent the summer in Wyoming learning how to use pitons, the metal spikes that climbers pound into rocks to secure their ropes. He hung out at prime climbing spots such as Stoney Point, Tahquitz Rock, and Gannett Peak—the tallest mountain in Wyoming. There was only one major problem: Despite his love of climbing, Yvon couldn't find any gear he truly liked. He wished that someday he could create his own.

A SERENDIPITOUS SOLUTION

Back in Southern California, Yvon's later teenage years were filled with stops and starts. He tried community college but eventually quit going to his classes. He got a job as a private detective at an agency run by his older brother, but the gig was short lived. Mostly, he hung out with more experienced climbers he met at the Sierra Club, such as T. M. Herbert, Royal Robbins, and Tom Frost. The crew often went to Yosemite, a national park renowned for its towering cliffs, to hone and perfect their skills.

In 1957, when Yvon was 19, the dream of making the perfect climbing gear became a reality. First, he bought a secondhand anvil and forge and set up a station in his backyard to do blacksmithing work. His father helped him build a workspace out of an old chicken coop. Yvon's parents also lent him $825 so he could buy more tools. After his first few rounds of blacksmithing pitons and carabiners, the D-shaped metal clips used by rock climbers to hold freely running rope, he tried them out himself. He visited climbing spots from Lost Arrow Chimney and the north face of Sentinel Rock in Yosemite to the Shawangunk Mountains in New York.

Before long, Yvon's friends and acquaintances wanted some of his creations for their own. At first, he made

THE REALIZED ULTIMATE REALITY PITON (RURP)

In 1960, the only piton available on the market was the knifeblade, a hardened-steel, removable model designed by Yosemite climber Chuck Wilts. It came in different sizes. But it bent under pressure. It also broke when hammered too fiercely, a disaster waiting to happen for any rock climber. The soon-to-be founders of Chouinard Equipment, Yvon Chouinard and Tom Frost, set out to solve the problem. They started by breaking apart hacksaw blades and creating pitons out of the ground-out saw teeth. The results were too thin and brittle. Next, they took a blade of chromium molybdenum, a type of alloy used in aircraft production, heated it, then pounded it out to size. The process was too expensive. Finally, they used the same materials but molded them into a postage stamp–sized piton with a tiny hole. This time, the experiment worked. Chouinard and Frost christened their design the Realized Ultimate Reality Piton (RURP).

just enough equipment to support his massive climbing habit. He sold the gear out of the back of his car during climbing trips. He could make two pitons per hour, and he sold them for $1.50 each.[2]

Then in 1966, Yvon moved his blacksmith shop to a tin shed behind a slaughterhouse in Ventura, California. He had partnered with Frost, who had become an aeronautical engineer, and Frost's wife to form a climbing company called Chouinard Equipment. They were inspired by a quote from French aviator and author Antoine de Saint-Exupéry: "In anything at all, perfection is finally attained not when there is no longer anything to add, but when there is no longer anything to take away, when a body has been stripped down to its nakedness."[3] In their nine-year partnership, Chouinard and the Frosts made it their mission to craft the lightest, strongest, and most durable climbing equipment on the market.

CHANGE IN COURSE

By the early 1970s, Chouinard Equipment was raking in sales, with profits of more than $400,000 a year.[4] It sold everything from ice axes to crampons, the metal spikes that attach to footwear and help trekkers gain traction. The business grew to become the largest supplier of

> *Chouinard's original tin shed still stands today.*

climbing equipment in the United States. "Yvon was the idea man, I was the engineer," Frost told *Climbing* magazine in 2009.[5] But in spite of its huge success, the company's focus was shifting. Chouinard had begun to realize that the pitons that made up 70 percent of his

"CLEAN" CLIMBING

Chouinard Equipment's 1972 catalog was revolutionary in more ways than one. It was not only the first catalog for the climbing company, but it was also the first publication to bring the environmental impact of the sport into the spotlight and offer solutions on how to be cleaner climbers. Within months of the catalog's mailing, nearly everyone had switched from using pitons to using chocks. "No longer can we assume the earth's resources are limitless; that there are ranges of unclimbed peaks extending endlessly beyond the horizon. Mountains are finite, and despite their massive appearance, they are fragile," Chouinard and Frost wrote in the 14-page essay at the front of the catalog. "We can offer a few immediate solutions. Stay off climbs you do not intend to finish. . . . Do not use artificial aid on free climbs. But most of all, start using chocks."[7]

business were destructive to the environment.[6] Using them to climb left rocks pitted with minuscule holes, which eventually caused the rocks to crack, crumble, and deteriorate.

To combat the problem head on, Chouinard and Frost made one essential change. Instead of merely creating the best, lightest, and most effective climbing gear available, Chouinard Equipment would now also consider environmental responsibility. In 1972, the company produced its first catalog. It included a 14-page essay that warned climbers about the environmental impact of their sport. The company also started making lightweight aluminum

> *The unique needs of climbers drove the innovation of Chouinard Equipment's early years.*

PRODUCT SPOTLIGHT

THE SENDER

Chouinard's favorite rugby shirt didn't originate as a climbing shirt. The style of shirt was originally used as part of a uniform for rugby players in the United Kingdom as early as the 1830s. The shirts were made of wool and paired with white trousers.

When Chouinard picked up his rugby pullover in Scotland in 1970, it was made out of a more heavyweight and breathable cotton fabric, making it perfect for climbing. It had a contrast-color fold-down collar that protected climbers' necks from rope burn. The style surged in popularity in the 1970s. Climbers from coast to coast bought the shirts from Chouinard Equipment and later Patagonia.

In 2015, Patagonia brought back the style with a refreshed silhouette, calling it the Sender shirt. It was made of heavy-duty organic cotton jersey fabric with a straight hem, twill collar, and three rubber buttons. It came in both short- and long-sleeve versions, in gray, rust, or blue. The shirt was priced at $62. On one retail website, the Sender was listed along with the tagline: "This shirt has the ability to stand up to the roughest grit stone in the Peaks and the comfort to while away the afternoons in the pub."[8]

nuts to replace the original steel pitons. These devices, called chocks, could be inserted into cracks already present in rocks and then be attached to ropes to anchor a climber. The chocks could be easily removed after an ascent or descent, leaving the rocks damage-free.

In 1970, something happened that altered the course of Chouinard's business once again. While on a climbing trip in Scotland, he bought a rugby shirt that was blue with two red stripes and one yellow stripe across the chest. The shirt was heavyweight and durable. It was also surprisingly breathable to wear during climbing sessions. Its polo-style collar prevented Chouinard's gear from scratching his neck during ascents or rappels.

Chouinard practically lived in the shirt when he got back to the United States. He also started importing other versions to sell under the Chouinard Equipment brand. The move was so profitable that he branched out into other areas, such as selling shorts and gloves. Before long, clothing and accessories sales overtook sales of the climbing equipment. Chouinard was overjoyed. What began as a makeshift blacksmith shop inside a former chicken coop would soon become one of the most well-respected outdoor clothing brands in the world.

CHAPTER THREE

THE BIRTH OF PATAGONIA

By the early 1970s, Chouinard had come a long way from his days as a young boy who clung to the falconry club as a respite from everyday life. As an adult, he had fully immersed himself in the wonders of climbing, exploring the unknown, and going on outdoor excursions. Along with a ragtag group of other adventurers, including accomplished mountaineer Rick Ridgeway, Chouinard zigzagged across the world in search of the next mighty peak to conquer.

Matching his insatiable appetite for adventure, Chouinard's desire to expand his business grew. At the end of 1972, Chouinard Equipment still sold climbing tools. But sales of its bare-bones clothing line outpaced sales of its climbing

> *Chouinard at a Patagonia production facility in Santa Barbara, California*

BLACK DIAMOND EQUIPMENT

When Chouinard and Frost started Chouinard Equipment in 1965, they focused solely on selling climbing gear. But when a portion of the company splintered off to form Patagonia, hardware sales declined. This, along with Patagonia's rapid expansion, the massive outflow of cash to keep the company running, and the constant race to fill orders in a timely fashion, caused trouble for Chouinard. Eventually, the business couldn't keep up, and in 1989 Chouinard filed for bankruptcy. He laid off 120 employees—a fifth of his workforce.[1] A group of former Chouinard Equipment employees bought the equipment portion of the company and moved it to Salt Lake City, Utah. They renamed it Black Diamond Equipment. Many of Chouinard's designs are still sold under that label today.

inventory. By then, the ground level of the old slaughterhouse in Ventura had been transformed into a retail shop. The upstairs was where many of the products were sewn and packaged to be sold. Little by little, the company added more products to its repertoire, including other rugby shirts from England, rain jackets and bivouac sacks from Scotland, wool gloves from Austria, and hand-knit reversible beanies from Boulder, Colorado.

The success in selling apparel inspired Chouinard; his wife, Malinda; and the Frosts to do something bold. In 1973, they officially formed a new outdoor apparel and accessories company. They decided to call it Patagonia, after the vast mountainous region Chouinard loved to climb in Argentina and Chile. Now all the fledgling business needed was some effective marketing and an eye-catching, instantly identifiable logo.

CLIMBING A GIANT

A RUGGED IMAGE

In order to come up with a suitable logo, Chouinard didn't have to look too far for inspiration. Up until that point, his entire life had been about climbing. He had named his company Patagonia. Why not create a logo to match? The final design resembled Fitz Roy, a mountain in Patagonia. Fitz Roy is one of the toughest mountains to climb in the world. Chouinard himself had summitted it just a few years earlier.

For Chouinard, Patagonia's logo matched the company's philosophy perfectly. It symbolized the business's adventurous spirit and emphasized spending time in nature. It also advertised the products' durability and strength. One early example of this durability was the aptly named Stand Up shorts, suitable for multiday treks,

In 1968, Chouinard took one of the most legendary trips of his lifetime. Along with three other climbers, Doug Tompkins, Dick Dorworth, and Chris Jones, he road-tripped from his home in California to the border between Chile and Argentina in the Patagonia wilderness. The goal was to climb Fitz Roy, one of the most impressive and death-defying ascents on the face of the earth. In addition to accomplishing the amazing feat, the crew filmed their journey. Along the way, they sand skied in the desert and spent 31 days in an ice cave. Portions of the film were released to the public as a documentary entitled *Mountain of Storms* and another film called *Fitz Roy*. The movies not only showcased the climbers' quest for greatness but also highlighted the origin story behind Patagonia's name and philosophy as a company.

> *Patagonia's logo evokes the rocky region for which the brand was named.*

risky climbing ascents, and even bouldering. Made from tough canvas, the shorts were so intentionally stiff that they could stand up by themselves.

Another example was the pile fleece jacket, first released in 1977. It was modeled after the hardy clothing worn by fishermen. It had a high, stand-up collar to protect the neck. At the time, many mountaineering companies were constructing outdoor clothing out of cotton, wool, and down feathers. Contrary to this approach, Patagonia used synthetic material. This meant it could insulate without absorbing moisture—two essential qualities of a cold-weather garment.

But Patagonia's early years as a company weren't all filled with inspirational moments and product successes. Not long after the company got up and running, it hit a significant obstacle. A factory in Hong Kong sent Chouinard a large quantity of poorly made rugby shirts to stock the shelves. Many of the shirts had defects. All of them shrank when washed. Customers were furious, and many demanded a refund. The company nearly went bankrupt as a result. Chouinard later wrote in his book, "We learned the hard way that there was a big difference between running a blacksmith shop and being in the rag business."[2] As a result of the Hong Kong debacle, Chouinard's relationship with his business partners soured. The Frosts sold the Chouinards their share

A SPORT-CHANGING MATERIAL

Patagonia's pile jackets are known for their softness and warming qualities. But creating such a product wasn't easy. The company's first run of similarly styled clothing was made of fabric that was supposed to be used for toilet-seat covers. When looking for ways to make the next iteration of the design, the product team searched high and low for other options. Finally, Malinda, Chouinard's wife, hit the jackpot. She went to Malden Mills in Los Angeles, an outpost of a Massachusetts textile manufacturer that specialized in baby bunting, and found synthetic pile. When she brought some back to the office, the design team whipped up a sample jacket to field-test in freezing conditions. The experiment worked. Unlike cotton, pile still insulated when wet. It also dried quickly. Best of all, it was so warm that it reduced the bulky layers a climber or hiker had to wear.

of the company in 1975, leaving Yvon and Malinda as its sole owners.

FIRST FORAY INTO ENVIRONMENTAL ADVOCACY

From its early days, Patagonia made a point to stay involved in its community of climbers, hikers, kayakers, and outdoors enthusiasts. Even as its business weathered hiccups and grew more successful, company employees continued to solicit the public for feedback on products and ask for suggestions on new innovations. They made an effort to be as transparent as possible about how the company's products were made.

Chouinard and Patagonia's workers also kept track of issues pertaining to the environment. One of their first ventures took place in 1972. A group of Patagonia staff joined forces with Mark Capelli, a young graduate student and environmental activist. He was protesting the looming construction of a concrete channel and a freeway-related commercial development at the mouth of the Ventura River, near Patagonia's offices. If the project were approved, the channel would not only disrupt a popular surf break but also harm the environment. The river was instrumental to a number of wildlife species

LIFELONG FRIENDS

living in the estuary, including birds, water snakes, muskrats, and raccoons. Before the previous construction of two dams had diverted the river in a different spot farther upstream, the corridor had once been a major steelhead trout habitat. Capelli argued the river should be allowed to flow naturally to protect as many aquatic and land species as possible.

Yvon Chouinard and Tom Frost ended their business partnership in 1975. Despite their cut ties, the two remained friends until Frost died on August 24, 2018. Throughout their lives, the men conquered great heights together. They founded and ran Chouinard Equipment for a decade. They also made the first ascent of the North America wall of El Capitan, a massive rock formation in Yosemite, in 1964. When Frost died, Patagonia posted a moving eulogy on its company website: "For all he did, Tom was noted for his humility, a low-key style and egalitarian presence in the workplace. He will be deeply missed by those who had the pleasure to work with him. His legacy lives on in everyone who climbs."[3]

Some Patagonia staffers accompanied Capelli to a city council meeting to try to prevent the project. Thanks in part to their public outcry, the development plans never went through. The victory led to the expansion of the Friends of Ventura River action group. Chouinard gave Capelli and his colleagues some office space and extra funding to help them clean up the Ventura River.

The Ventura River campaign was the first major environmental activism victory for the Patagonia team.

FRIENDS OF THE VENTURA RIVER TODAY

Friends of the Ventura River, the innovative group that was born out of Patagonia and Mark Capelli's combined efforts to prevent the construction of a concrete channel in the river in 1974, has long since changed hands in leadership. But the organization's original mission and ethics still remain. Today, the much larger group is made up of community members and organizations such the Ventura Audubon Society, Los Padres Forest Watch, the Santa Barbara Channelkeeper, and Ojai Valley Green Coalition. These groups work together to restore the river and come up with sustainable ways to protect the area. Over the years, Patagonia has continued to sponsor their efforts.

It would not be the last. For more than four decades, the company continued to weigh in on important national and global issues. As one journalist for the *Seattle Times* wrote in 2018, "For more than 45 years, [Patagonia] has mixed business and politics to a degree unusual in corporate America. While companies are expected to weigh in on everything from gun control to transgender rights these days—and many do so uncomfortably—

Patagonia has been unapologetically political since the 1970s. It bills itself 'the Activist Company' and publicly advocates for [a myriad of news-making topics, such as] environmental protection, fair trade and stricter labor standards."[4]

> *A campaign to protect the Ventura River was among Patagonia's earliest environmental projects.*

CHAPTER FOUR

A CLOTHING REVOLUTION

By 1980, Chouinard was going through extraordinary changes in his life. His marriage was going well, and he had kids to take care of. He began cutting back on his climbing. In 1981, he and a few other climbing buddies were involved in an expedition on a peak called Gongga Shan in China. The group got caught in an avalanche. One climber died. The rest were badly injured. From that point forward, Chouinard sought out less risky adventures.

Chouinard also had more corporate responsibilities to manage. Business was booming for Patagonia, and it showed no sign of slowing down. Annual revenue shot up from $20 million in the mid-1980s to $100 million in 1990.[1]

> *Over time Chouinard focused less on his own outdoor adventures and more on managing the rapidly growing business.*

A DOGGED LEADER

Starting and sustaining a clothing company can be tricky. Many entrepreneurs fail. For example, American Apparel was an ethical clothing brand that became hugely popular in the early 2000s. Though it still has an online presence, the company is nowhere near as successful as it once was. Its notoriously free-spending founder, Dov Charney, has filed for bankruptcy twice. In contrast, much of Patagonia's success can be attributed to Chouinard's vision, generosity, and drive. Friends and business associates call him an icon. "I think he's one of the major figures of his generation. He's had a lot of effect on a lot of people. He's very generous," said Bruce Hill, a former logger turned fishing guide and conservationist. "He's [also] ruthlessly honest. He doesn't care a lot of times about making people uncomfortable."[3]

For Chouinard, it was clear he was doing something right. "I wanted to distance myself as far as possible from those pasty-faced corpses in suits I saw in airline magazine ads," Chouinard wrote in his book. "If I had to be a businessman, I was going to do it in my own terms."[2]

Patagonia had grown successful in part because of Chouinard's vision as a leader. But it also had to do with the company's standing as a brand. Patagonia developed a reputation for its inventive thinking in terms of materials and manufacturing. The company wasn't just churning out the same old designs and replicating other outdoor brands. It was revolutionizing the way active clothing and gear looked, felt, and functioned.

INNOVATIVE FIRSTS

From the very beginning, Patagonia snubbed fast fashion, the concept of clothing that could be worn today and discarded tomorrow. Instead, the company aimed to create products that stood the test of time. Updated versions of products from the company's early days are still on Patagonia stores' shelves today.

As the company aged, it became known for its innovative firsts. In 1980, Patagonia's designers experimented with polypropylene, a type of synthetic fiber that doesn't absorb water and was initially used for making marine ropes and the lining of disposable diapers. Instead of constructing base layers out of heavyweight cotton—which absorbs moisture, takes a long time to dry, and traps dampness next to the skin in chilly conditions—they tried polypropylene instead. The result was a game changer. Consumers loved the move away from cotton and wool. Sales of Patagonia's thermal underwear line made of polypropylene skyrocketed.

In 1981, the company was also the first of the outdoor brands to introduce brighter colors in its catalogs and on its store racks. It did not rely on the usual forest greens, tans, and charcoal grays of the industry's status quo.

SPORTS FOCUS

LAYER WITH PURPOSE

When participating in any sport, whether it's running a marathon or windsurfing, it's essential to have the right gear, including clothing. But how do shoppers figure out which garments are best for each situation? How do they prepare for a change in weather or body temperature? As soon as Patagonia started making thermal underwear using polypropylene in 1980, it knew it could educate people about layering.

> *Layering is crucial for those who participate in cold-weather sports and activities so they can stay warm and dry.*

Through essays in its catalogs, Patagonia became the first company to teach the importance of layering to the outdoor community. It called the first level a base layer. This inner layer should be worn against the skin for moisture management. Examples include Patagonia's thermal shirts, leggings, or underwear. The middle layer is worn for insulation. It keeps the wearer warm, even in freezing conditions. Examples include Patagonia's Nano Puff Jacket or its full-zip Better Sweater Vest. The outer layer, such as a light shell or windbreaker, is worn for protection against the wind and rain. It keeps the wearer's inner layers dry. Examples include Patagonia's Torrentshell 3L Jacket or its Dual Aspect Jacket.

When worn all together as a system, these layers will keep an athlete or outdoor enthusiast not only warm and dry but energized and comfortable too. If the weather shifts, a layer can easily be added or dropped to suit the circumstances.

> *Patagonia carries clothing in both the traditional muted colors of outdoor clothes and a variety of bolder hues.*

Instead, it made sweaters in cobalt blue, socks in teal and seafoam green, full-zip jackets in red, and puffer coats in mocha brown. "Traditionally gear had been drab and austere, dominated by muted browns, greens and beiges," apparel writer Brenden Gallagher noted. "Intelligently catering to both popular culture and its dedicated group of climbers, Patagonia changed all that by releasing its products in bold colors."[4]

One of Patagonia's most popular inventions during the early 1980s combined Chouinard's love of surfing with his quest to manufacture the ideal pair of shorts that were durable but not quite as rugged as the Stand-Up model. In 1982, the Baggies hit the market. These shorts, which came in two different inseams, quickly developed a cult following due to their durability and comfort. Made of water-repellent nylon, they could be worn for a range of outdoor activities, from hiking and trail running to waterskiing and stand-up paddle boarding.

RESEARCH AND DESIGN

As was the case for many burgeoning outdoor gear companies of the 1980s and 1990s, one reason for Patagonia's rapid rise in fame and increased sales had to do with its emphasis on field-testing each and every one of its products. At the same time, the company also poured money into research and development to solve any problems that arose with its products' designs. It paid specific attention to fixing common issues such as pilling on a sweater, odor retention in socks, or easily ripped fabric on hiking pants.

During this thorough test-and-review process, many fashion breakthroughs occurred. For example, in

REAL-WORLD PRODUCT TESTING

Like many mountaineering outfitters, Patagonia relies on field research and rigorous analysis to ensure its products are the best they can be. Athletes and people Patagonia calls ambassadors put the latest designs and fabrics to the test in real-life situations before products ever make it to the catalog or shelves. Climbers scale mountains to see if their Patagonia pants rip or develop holes. Campers and kayakers wear Patagonia's Capilene underwear in sub-freezing temperatures to see if their core stays warm. If problems arise, the design gets tweaked until the testers are satisfied. But just because a product is available for sale doesn't mean the testing period is over. Patagonia relies on its customer base to provide ongoing feedback, whether negative or positive, so improvements can still be made if needed.

1984 Chouinard attended a sporting goods trade show in Chicago, Illinois. There, he watched a demonstration by a company called Milliken about polyester football jerseys. The jerseys' fabric was made of tiny hydrophilic ridges that wicked moisture away from the wearer's skin. Chouinard thought it would make the perfect material for Patagonia's base layer line. He took home a sample and gave it to the research and development team. It went through rigorous field-testing. A year later, cutting-edge Capilene polyester was born. Chouinard retired the entire polypropylene line in favor of making Patagonia's base layers out of Capilene.

The shift was a big risk. The items made out of polypropylene represented 70 percent of Patagonia's sales.[5] But the brand's customer base immediately latched on to the new fabric because of its smooth feel and insulating qualities. Sales jumped once more.

By 1993, Patagonia, like many companies, had become aware of an increasing problem that was impacting the environment: plastic waste. In response, its research and development team created a product that could not only address that issue but look great too. The company produced the outdoor clothing world's first fleece fabric made from recycled content. By recycling 25 plastic bottles and turning them into a material called polyethylene terephthalate (PET), it could create one fleece product.[6] A more ecologically friendly version of the brand's Synchilla fleece material, PET was used to make the Retro-X recycled fleece line and an updated version of the iconic Patagonia Snap-T pullover.

Toward the end of the 1990s, Patagonia introduced yet another breakthrough product: the Storm jacket. It was made with the company's H2No waterproof fabric, which could withstand downpours and blustery conditions. The company hired snowboarders, rock climbers, and hikers, asking them to wear the jacket while doing their sport. After many rounds of feedback, H2No waterproof fabric has been continuously tweaked and updated to reduce its environmental impact and improve performance.

PRODUCT SPOTLIGHT

THE SNAP-T PULLOVER

In 1981, Chouinard and the owner of Malden Mills, Aaron Feuerstein, collaborated on a new type of fleece fabric. Called Synchilla, which stands for synthetic chinchilla, it combined insulation with performance. The fabric also wicked away moisture.

In 1985, Patagonia used Synchilla in its new Snap-T pullover. Skiers, snowboarders, and hikers across the United States and the world bought the garment in droves. It had two kangaroo pockets in the front and a stand-up collar with snaps up the neck for added protection. The Synchilla material became synonymous with fleece. "For many, many years," says Rob Bondurant, vice president of marketing at Patagonia, "Synchilla was the Kleenex of fleece."[7]

Since its first run, the Snap-T and its fabric have gone through many revisions. By 1993, Patagonia had started making it out of recycled content. At first, customers complained that the fleece felt scratchy. It also pilled. But after further refinements, the new recycled version was lighter and less susceptible to pilling, and it could be made at a fraction of the cost of the original.

> *Patagonia's waterproof jackets are a key part of its product line.*

The material is still used in Patagonia's waterproof jackets to this day.

Since its inception, Patagonia has become known for its enduring product designs and its commitment to the environment. But there are other reasons people rally behind the brand. Some people apply for jobs there not only for easy access to products such as Storm jackets and Snap-T pullovers but also to be a part of Patagonia's inclusive work environment.

PATAGONIA: AT THE OFFICE

P atagonia has become one of the world's largest and most respected outdoor outfitters. What started out as a tin shed in Chouinard's backyard with one lone employee is now a major international presence with offices, factories, and stores scattered across the globe. Alex Rakestraw of fashion website Highsnobiety notes, "Patagonia is the rare brand with its own center of gravity. An iconic logo. A telegraphed purpose. Behind it all, a dogmatic focus on doing things right. . . . This singularity of purpose (alongside some brilliant products, of course) has made Patagonia one of the most well-known brands in all of techwear."[1]

> *Patagonia's corporate headquarters are located in Ventura, California.*

A MAFIA MISS

Throughout the 1980s, Patagonia was growing rapidly. More retail stores were being built. Consumers kept buying its products. But around 1991, a recession hit. Banks stopped lending money so freely. It affected Patagonia's bottom line. "We had bought inventory for another 50 percent growth and as it turned out we only had a 30 percent growth," recalled Chouinard. "Well, that's a huge difference. And we got into a really deep financial trouble. I mean so deep that I could hardly get out of it."

Chouinard said his accountants introduced him to the mafia, a criminal organization, so he could ask them for a loan. In the end, he didn't go through with it. Instead, he borrowed the money from friends. "[It] was a wake-up call that I was doing business just like everybody else," Chouinard said. "I was growing for the sake of growing and not thinking about what I was doing. And that forced us to sit down, all of us in the company and ask ourselves why are we in business."[3]

But Patagonia's record hasn't always been so stellar. In fact, after the brand's financial success throughout the 1980s, the company suffered a number of setbacks, some of which were severe. For example, during a 1991 economic decline, Patagonia overextended itself monetarily. As a result, it laid off about 120 employees, nearly 20 percent of its Ventura staff.[2] The employees were from all parts of the company, from upper management and sales directors to cafeteria workers and the janitorial team. "It's a recognition that we tried to grow too fast as a company," spokesman Kevin Sweeney said at the time. "We had projected much larger growth, but we finally realized what the ceiling is. The market has told us not to grow."[4]

Despite the hiccup, Patagonia slowly returned to its former status as the economy recovered. For the next 30 years, it continued to grow and attract more employees. One of the chief reasons so many people want to work there is the company culture.

EMPLOYEES COME FIRST

In keeping with Patagonia's ethos of maintaining ecologically sound and forward-thinking business practices, Chouinard built a company that has supported its employees' well-being whenever possible. In 1983, thanks to Malinda Chouinard's urging, it became one of the first companies in the United States to provide on-site childcare for its employees. New parents received generous time off, employees got sick leave, and they even received paid time off for environmental internships. Two years later, Patagonia built the Great Pacific Child Development Center for employees' families. By 2015, the center had expanded to cover more than 12,000 square feet (1,115 sq m), with outdoor space, fruit trees, and 28 staff members.[5] That same year, Patagonia was recognized by President Barack Obama for its commitment to

MALINDAGRAMS

Yvon Chouinard is the main face of Patagonia. But his wife, Malinda, plays an important role behind the scenes. According to Yvon, she is the person responsible for making the company a fun, innovative, and impeccably organized place to work. "Malinda is much more involved than I am," he told the New Yorker. "She's more of a micromanager."[7]

One of the ways Malinda keeps the staff on track is by sending out messages that have become known as Malindagrams. These email blasts go out to all the staff. They include motivations for the week, information on new initiatives, and directives on other employee-related matters in the company.

working families. "We've raised fifteen hundred kids so far," Chouinard told a reporter from the New Yorker.[6]

In 1984, Patagonia opened an on-site cafeteria for employees at its Ventura headquarters. It served healthy food for a wide range of diets, with a particular focus on providing organic options. At the end of each shift, cafeteria staff composted the kitchen waste instead of throwing it in the trash.

That same year, Patagonia did away with private offices altogether. In their place, executives decided on an open floor plan to foster communication and collaboration. Instead of having cubicles assigned to them, employees could work wherever they chose to sit or stand for the day, whether at a desk, on a couch, or even outside. After work or

> *Since the 1980s, Patagonia has gained a reputation as a laid-back, relaxed place to work.*

WORKPLACE STATS

In 2019, Patagonia ranked Number 100 in *Fortune* magazine's Top 100 places to work in the United States. It had made the honorary mentions list five times before that. According to the magazine, people love working there. Several reasons were given. One hundred percent of employees' health care is covered by the company, including that of part-time workers. There is a gym on-site, as well as a childcare center with a bilingual staff. Employees receive 18 paid days off and 9 sick days per year, and can take a fully paid sabbatical. A portion of college tuition is also reimbursed by the company. More than 31,000 people applied for jobs with Patagonia in 2019 alone.[9]

during breaks, they could play volleyball on the outdoor sandpit behind the building, go surfing, or go for a run on nearby trails. The company also sponsored skiing, climbing, and trekking trips in California's Sierra Nevada mountains.

That same laid-back but dedicated attitude continues to hold true. As one might guess, the office dress code is generally casual. Workers often show up wearing their own Patagonia gear. Some even walk around the office barefoot. But the work always gets done. "Our management system is kind of like an ant colony . . . [There are] no bosses in an ant colony but every single ant knows what his job is and gets it done," says Chouinard. "That's our management style. And so I hire very independent, very self-motivated people who believe in what we're trying to do and I leave them alone."[8]

A RESPONSIBLE SUPPLY CHAIN

As a rapidly growing company, Patagonia didn't focus solely on keeping its employees happy over the years. It also made great strides in other areas, such as monitoring the working conditions in its retail stores and supply chains and keeping track of where and how its money was being spent. In 1985, Patagonia donated 10 percent of its annual profits to environmental groups.[10] Over the years, the practice evolved to a donation of 10 percent of its annual revenue or 1 percent of its total sales, whichever figure turned out to be higher. Officially nicknamed "1% for the Planet" in 2002, and sometimes known as the "Earth Tax," this practice remains in place. The company has given more than $140 million in cash and in-kind donations to national and

THE CONSERVATION ALLIANCE

From the beginning, Patagonia has been a company with an eye toward activism and environmental awareness. In 1989, it helped form an organization that aimed to protect outdoor spaces by inspiring major companies and communities to work together toward this common goal. Called the Conservation Alliance, the group now consists of more than 260 member companies, including REI, The North Face, and Kelty. The group has given away more than $27 million. It has helped protect wetlands and rivers, stop or remove harmful dams, designate five marine reserves, and purchase 21 climbing areas. In 2021 alone, the alliance gave away more than $2 million.[11]

international environmental groups.[12] "It's real. It's not a story. It's not strategy. It's a real human thing," said Craig Wilson, a former Patagonia employee who worked in the company's marketing and digital department.[13]

In 1990, Patagonia's Quality Assurance (QA) team took a closer look at the company's manufacturing partners. They wanted to make sure production levels remained high on an ongoing basis, but they also wanted to ensure factory conditions were ethically sound and that workers weren't being pushed to their breaking point. In order to make that happen, they issued a statement that Patagonia would no longer work with any factory the QA team couldn't visit in person. In-person visits were important to make sure factory employees were being treated fairly. By the mid-1990s, Patagonia had contracted with third-party auditors to monitor and track all of its factories to ensure their policies were up to par.

In addition to constantly revamping and updating its ethical and financial initiatives, Patagonia also tracked its impact on the environment. In 1996, it opened a large new distribution and customer service center in Reno, Nevada. Unlike the company's headquarters, which was

> *Engineers at Patagonia headquarters develop new designs and methods for making clothes.*

THE FAIR LABOR ASSOCIATION

In the mid-1990s, Patagonia sought a way to monitor and investigate potential abusive labor practices in its factories and manufacturing partners. In 1996, its executives met with those from other companies such as Adidas and Nike at the White House to come up with a plan to improve working conditions in the apparel and footwear industry. A three-year process led to the formation of the Fair Labor Association (FLA) in 1999. "Today's agreement on fighting sweatshop practices is an historic step toward reducing sweatshop labor around the world and will give American consumers confidence that the clothes they buy are made under decent and humane working conditions," President Clinton said at the time.[14] Still in existence today, the FLA has expanded to include universities and civil society organizations as partners. It audits factories, provides training, and aims to improve the lives of workers across the globe.

initially constructed out of unsustainable materials such as wood from old-growth trees—a choice Chouinard has said he regrets—this building would serve as an environmentally responsible model for the future. The company set a goal to achieve a significant reduction in energy use by installing solar-tracking skylights and heating that radiated down from panels on the ceiling. It used recycled or reclaimed content for everything from the carpet on the floor to the dividers between urinals in the men's bathrooms. Patagonia matched this effort in its retail stores. For example, it retrofitted lighting systems by swapping out inefficient lightbulbs with more environmentally responsible models that used less energy.

60

That same year, the company signed on to President Bill Clinton's No Sweat Initiative, which set the minimum standards for working conditions in corporate supply chains. In 2002, the company hired a social responsibility manager who was in charge of overseeing and handling major problems within the company's supply chain. At the same time, Patagonia employees were given training on how to work more efficiently and effectively in order to reduce any unintended pressure on factory workers. By the mid-2000s, the company was well on its way to becoming one of the top players in the outdoor outfitter arena.

CHAPTER SIX

THE DO-GOOD COMPANY

As a company, Patagonia puts a premium on how its products stand up, not just in terms of their durability but also in terms of their environmental footprint. It earned much of its reputation for being a responsible and forward-thinking company by figuring out how to fix the mistakes it made along the way. For example, in 1988, Patagonia opened a retail store in Boston, Massachusetts. Soon after employees stocked the shelves with Patagonia products, they started experiencing headaches. An investigation determined the cause was inadequate ventilation, coupled with toxic formaldehyde fumes coming from the clothing. The fumes were remnants of the manufacturing process. This prompted

> *Solar panels at its corporate headquarters are one visible demonstration of Patagonia's environmental commitments.*

a multiyear study to determine how to create outdoor gear in a healthier, more sustainable fashion.

The results of the study were extraordinary, especially with regard to cotton. According to Patagonia's findings, cotton fields make up 2.5 percent of the world's cultivated land. But cotton cultivation accounts for 22.5 percent of the chemical insecticides and 10 percent of the pesticides used in agriculture.[1] Not only are these insecticides and pesticides harmful to the environment and a major source of pollution, but they are also harmful to the consumers who buy cotton products.

In response, Patagonia set a goal to use 100 percent organic cotton in all of its cotton products by 1996. "The shift to organic cotton was our first sustained and widespread effort to change our supply chain," wrote Michele Bianchi, who was the managing editor for Patagonia content at the time. "It was also the first time we ran a company-wide environmental initiative and created an internal and external environmental educational campaign."[2]

COMPANY-WIDE INITIATIVES

After Patagonia's cotton incident, executives implemented a series of initiatives over the next two decades to make

THE ORGANIC COTTON SNAP-T PULLOVER

PRODUCT SPOTLIGHT

The Organic Cotton Snap-T pullover is a heritage-inspired version of Patagonia's Snap-T pullover. It is made of 100 percent organic cotton fabric and is diamond-quilted for texture and warmth. It has a contrast-color flap pocket on the left chest and a stand-up collar. The pocket and inner collar are made of 100 percent recycled nylon plain weave with a durable water-repellent finish. The Organic Cotton Snap-T features Y-joint sleeves to allow for easy movement in the arms and shoulders. The shirt can be layered or worn on its own for hiking, boating, camping, or everyday use.

Patagonia started making this product out of organic cotton because organically farmed cotton avoids the use of toxic pesticides and herbicides. Instead, farmers use natural methods to manage bugs and create healthy soil. These methods also bring significant reductions in carbon dioxide emissions and water usage. In 2020, Patagonia went one step further. It launched a pilot program on partner farms to work toward Regenerative Organic Certification. This is the highest standard of organic certification. Its goal is to inspire farmers to grow organic cotton while regenerating the soil and improving the lives of animals and workers on the farm.

THE FOOTPRINT CHRONICLES

The Footprint Chronicles is a website that launched in 2007 and is constantly evolving. It allows consumers to trace the journey of the Patagonia products they buy, from their initial design through manufacturing and to store shelves. Customers can look at a world map, click on a pin, and find out information about the mills and factories that were used.

When Lisa Polley started working for Patagonia, she was excited about the access to sturdy, attractive outdoor gear. But when she got assigned to work on The Footprint Chronicles project, her life actually changed for the better. "Never have I experienced a project with such a direct impact on the company, on its employees and on myself as The Footprint Chronicles website," Polley said. "It's given me hope about the future for the first time in longer than I care to admit."[3]

sure its supply chain and corporate offices remained socially, environmentally, and fiscally responsible at all times. In 2006, it sharply reduced the number of factories the company used. This was meant to cut back on costs. But it also brought greater transparency to working conditions and ensured each factory met Patagonia's standards in its treatment of workers.

In 2010, Patagonia created a director of social and environmental responsibility position at its headquarters. This role oversaw the company's efforts to implement more sustainable practices and advance basic human rights in all aspects of its supply chain. That same year, Patagonia also partnered with the Environmental Protection Agency and companies such as Walmart to found the Sustainable

Apparel Coalition (SAC). This global nonprofit alliance was formed to hold apparel companies more accountable by measuring the environmental and social labor impacts of their products.

The following year, Patagonia ran its memorable and effective "Don't Buy This Jacket" ad campaign in the *New York Times* on Black Friday, the most popular shopping day of the year. It encouraged consumers to rethink their buying habits and avoid fast fashion. The ad directed shoppers to the newly formed Patagonia Common Threads Initiative (CTI), which asked customers to send back used Patagonia gear to be repaired and returned or resold instead of being thrown out.

In 2012, what started as a blog featuring customers' stories of appreciation about Patagonia products was transformed into a massive used clothing business called Worn Wear. Similar to CTI, Worn Wear promoted the responsible care, repair, reuse, resale, or recycling of a product at the end of its life. Patagonia employees staged pop-up events where customers could turn in their clothing in exchange for credit to use at a future date. They even had a mobile shop run by a small team that traveled the country and repaired people's clothing for free. In 2017, the company launched a fully online

> *In 2010, Patagonia partnered with the company Upcycle It Now to turn worn-out apparel into coats for dogs.*

version of Worn Wear. "The company's famous 'Don't Buy This Jacket' campaign drew attention to the issue of overconsumption, encouraging people to buy only what they need," wrote reporter Katherine Martinko for the sustainability website Treehugger. "The Worn Wear mission fits in well with that, reminding people that clothing can have a much longer life than what we sometimes think."[4]

CHANGING THE ENVIRONMENT, ONE GRASSROOTS EFFORT AT A TIME

In addition to maintaining a razor-sharp focus on responsible consumption, Chouinard and Patagonia talked about engaging in environmental activism and actually followed through with action. In 1988, the company launched its first national environmental campaign. The goal was to educate the public about deurbanizing the

FAIR TRADE CERTIFIED CLOTHING

All over the world, people work in factories in poor conditions and for low wages to create the clothing people rely on every day. In 2014, Patagonia partnered with Fair Trade USA to help put a dent in the problem. It pays factories a premium for any item that is Fair Trade Certified. The extra money goes directly to workers, who can put it toward community improvement projects, health-care programs, or even their daily groceries. Today, Patagonia sells more Fair Trade Certified items than any other apparel brand. The program has impacted more than 64,000 workers in ten countries around the globe.[6]

Yosemite Valley. Chouinard solicited essays from scientists, rangers, and writers about why things such as car pollution, hotel construction, and constant foot traffic were so harmful to the national park and surrounding area. He included them in Patagonia's catalogs and on posters throughout its retail stores.

In each year that followed, Patagonia chose a new education campaign on a major environmental issue to support. The campaigns ranged from public lands protection in Montana to a plastic bag ban in California. Some had successful conclusions, while others are still ongoing. "If you expect victories, then you're in the wrong business. Evil never stops. And it's just a matter of endless fighting," said Chouinard. "The fight is the important thing."[5]

In 2012, Patagonia became the first company in California to acquire benefit corporation status. This meant the company could legally stay mission driven as it grew in size and scope, rather than remaining strictly focused on financial returns for stockholders. A year later, it set up a fund designed to help finance start-ups with a focus on water conservation, organic agriculture, waste diversion, creating environmentally sustainable products, or building renewable energy infrastructure. The program has funded 12 startups and has given away more than $20 million.[7] In 2016, it gained the name Tin Shed Ventures after the original structure that had housed Chouinard Equipment. "We started the fund because we felt existing models for start-up capital were broken. Traditional investors tend to focus on short-term growth and profit, then quickly flip the companies in which they invest," the program's website explained. "We take a completely different approach to investing. We place environmental and social returns on equal footing with financial returns and provide long-term, patient capital that helps to support forward-thinking entrepreneurs for the long haul."[8]

Outside of carrying out grassroots campaigns and funding start-ups over the years, Patagonia made it a point to inform the public not only about its failures and successes but also about the inspiration for its business decisions. In 2005, Chouinard published *Let My People Go Surfing: The Education of a Reluctant Businessman*. Half memoir, half how-to guide, the book explores Chouinard's

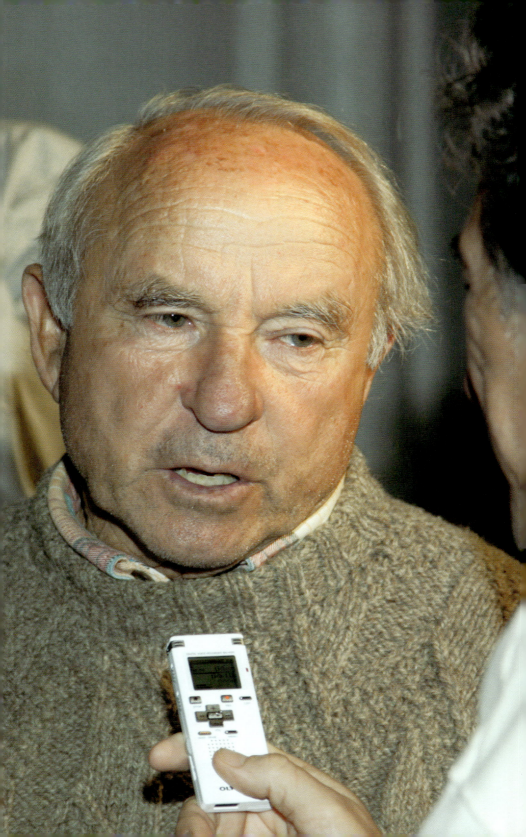

ACTIVISM IN PRINT

life and Patagonia's philosophy as a brand. The book was such a hit with consumers that the company decided to form its own publishing arm. Called Patagonia Books, its first title, *Yosemite in the Sixties* by Glen Denny, was published in 2007.

Since its launch, Patagonia Books has published more than 30 titles.[9] Many are written by the company's ambassadors, athletes, and outdoor gear nerds who test the brand's clothing and write essays for the catalogs. One percent of sales is donated to environmental charities through 1% for the Planet. "Part of the purpose of this program is to extend the message where the clothes can't go," said Patagonia Books director Karla Olsen.[10]

Through its publishing arm, Patagonia aims to share information with as many people as possible about crucial environmental, social, political, and ethical issues facing the world today. Two of its most popular books are *The Responsible Company*, by Chouinard and Vincent Stanley, and *Tools for Grassroots Activists*, by Patagonia staffers Nora Gallagher and Lisa Myers. The first, published in 2012, is a detailed account of the company and its stewardship efforts over 40 years. The second, published in 2016, is based on the Tools for Grassroots Activists Conference that Patagonia holds every two years. The conference teaches marketing, grassroots activism, and outreach skills to any of its workers who wish to attend. The book is a collection of the conferences' most enduring guidance and tips.

> *Chouinard has been open about the ups and downs of Patagonia's history.*

CHAPTER SEVEN

BRAND CONTROVERSIES

Patagonia's outspoken support of hot-button issues, including wildlife protection, Fair Trade Certified clothing, and increased transparency in apparel manufacturing, are well documented. Many of its campaigns and outreach efforts have been successful and sparked positive change both inside and outside the company. But in the brand's nearly 50 years of existence, there have been some pitfalls too. In fact, Patagonia has become embroiled in a number of thorny controversies since its founding. These controversies have centered on issues such as unethical working practices in its factories, overreach in its stewardship missions, and accusations of political meddling.

> *As with many other apparel companies, Patagonia has run into controversy around the facilities where its clothing is made.*

One major problem came to light in 2011. Cara Chacon and Thuy Nguyen, two managers involved in Patagonia's efforts on social responsibility, were doing an internal audit of the company to make sure everything was functioning smoothly. What they uncovered was shocking. According to their findings, Patagonia had instances of human trafficking and forced labor in its supply chain.

At the time, some of the textile mills Patagonia employed to create the fabric used in its clothing and gear were located in Taiwan. Many of these Taiwanese factories used labor brokers to find suitable workers. The brokers charged migrants illegally high sums of money, sometimes as much as $7,000, in exchange for jobs. Once hired, the workers had no freedom of movement. Their passports were taken away. They were also forced to pay a monthly fee to keep their jobs.

LABOR TRAFFICKING

Human trafficking in the labor market is a global problem. According to 2017 figures from the International Labor Office, an estimated 25 million people worldwide are trapped in forced labor conditions. Sixteen million of those people are in the private sector. The prevalence of forced labor is highest in Asia and the Pacific region, where four out of every 1,000 people are victims. This is followed by Europe and Central Asia (3.6 per 1,000), Africa (2.8 per 1,000), the Arab States (2.2 per 1,000), and the Americas (1.3 per 1,000). More women than men are affected by private forced labor. Approximately 9.2 million women and 6.8 million men are in this situation.[1]

By the end of each month, the workers were left with very little of their $630-a-month salary. "Labor trafficking is a huge problem globally. There really isn't any industry that is immune to this problem," says Agatha Tan, a senior adviser on labor trafficking at the advocacy group the Polaris Project.[2]

Patagonia mandated a new set of employment standards for migrant workers in 2015. It demanded that its factories reimburse workers for any fees above the legal limit that they were charged in order to get their jobs. At the time, it estimated that 5,000 workers would receive the money.[3] After June 1, 2015, Patagonia suppliers were required to eliminate hiring fees altogether.

When asked by a reporter from the *Atlantic* in 2015 about how consumers would react to the findings of worker exploitation in its supply chain, Patagonia executive Doug Freeman gave an honest response. "We think people will be disappointed, we think people will likely ask why we didn't do something sooner. We're going to be really honest about those things," he said. "We're going to dive very deeply into this issue and we're going to break trails for the rest of the industry."[4]

PATAGONIA'S PITFALLS

Patagonia's reputation as an outdoor outfitter is not perfect. In addition to the exploitation of workers in Taiwanese factories uncovered in 2011, a number of other issues have come to light over the years. In 2015, a study done by Greenpeace found Patagonia used toxic polyfluorinated chemicals (PFCs) to make some of its waterproof clothing. In response, the company released its first line of PFC-free waterproof gear. That same year, animal-rights organization PETA called out Patagonia for sourcing its wool from a farm in Argentina that treated its sheep poorly. The suppliers were immediately fired. Patagonia then created new standards for sourcing wool. From that point forward, all of its wool suppliers would need to be Responsible Wool Standard Certified and comply with Patagonia's criteria on animal welfare and sustainable land use.

PRESERVATION FOR A PURPOSE

Some companies and brands sought to steer clear of polarizing political issues, but Patagonia jumped right into these matters. Its website's "Activism" page noted that the company joined the fight on everything from trying to prevent oil drilling in the Great Australian Bight to asking the Tasmanian government to make the Tarkine Rainforest a protected World Heritage site. "We aim to use the resources we have—our voice, our business and our community—to do something about our climate crisis," the website explained.[5]

Many people see these efforts as necessary and show their support for the company's mission by buying its clothing and gear. "My experience with consumers, especially millennials, is that they are becoming more risk-averse when it comes to spending their money. They generally spend more carefully than previous generations," wrote Simonetta Lein, the founder of a charitable organization called the Wishwall Foundation. "However, when they do spend, there are some emerging patterns that favor sustainable brands. These consumers prefer to spend their money on brands that preach pro-social messages, apply sustainable manufacturing practices and exercise ethical business standards."[6]

Others were frustrated by the company's hands-on approach and see it as overreach. In 2018, during President Donald Trump's administration, Patagonia joined a number of Native American tribes and sued the government over its decision to drastically reduce the size of two national monuments in Utah: Bears Ears and Grand Staircase–Escalante. The company created its first-ever TV commercial to get the word out. "For as much authority as it gave to the president to create these monuments, Congress gave the president no authority to revoke or modify those monuments," the lawsuit read. "Congress is the sole authority that can undertake such changes."[7]

Republicans and Trump supporters were furious. They accused Patagonia of getting overtly political to sell more

> *Patagonia spoke out in favor of protecting Bears Ears National Monument in Utah.*

products. The hashtag #BoycottPatagonia went viral on Twitter. The Republican-controlled House Committee on Natural Resources weighed in on Twitter too. "Patagonia is lying to you," it tweeted. "A corporate giant hijacking our public lands debate to sell more products to wealthy elitist urban dwellers from New York to San Francisco."[8]

Patagonia has also long been involved in the highly controversial debate about whether certain hydroelectric

dams should continue to operate or be decommissioned to restore a river's natural flow and wildlife habitats. "I'm a fisherman, and I want to see fish come back to these rivers," Chouinard once said when asked about the issue. "I want to establish that when you put in a dam or when you dig an open-pit mine or scrape down a mountain, that you have to restore it. There's a public trust there and you have to restore it."[9]

In 2014, the company created *DamNation*, its first feature-length documentary, to educate the public about the problem. The film was produced by Patagonia and environmental assessment firm Stoecker Ecological in conjunction with the Colorado-based filmmaking team Felt Soul Media. It highlighted successful dam removals, called out dams that were the subject of ongoing removal debates, and shined a light on other dams that were, in the filmmakers' eyes, the perfect candidates for future demolition. Many people, especially those in the hydroelectric power industry, thought Patagonia was getting

NEW LOCALISM

In addition to being one of the world's top outdoor brands and running a small publishing company, Patagonia also dabbles in another medium: film. Beginning with *DamNation*, the company has created dozens of short and feature-length documentaries tackling everything from preventing resort development in British Columbia's Jumbo Valley (*Jumbo Wild*) to protesting offshore drilling near Santa Barbara off the California coast (*Crude Awakening*) to protecting Patagonia Park in Chile (*Mile for Mile*). As a collection, the films advocate a far-reaching idea on a small scale, a concept the company calls New Localism. Patagonia hopes to inspire people to solve the world's big problems by acting locally to solve the small ones. "The New Localism model, where we look at film and the voices of local activists and athletes, our people and community, has really enabled us to have a good technique for getting active around issues and nimble in a different sort of way," says Patagonia's campaigns and advocacy director, Hans Cole.[10]

> *This dam was removed from the Elwha River in Washington state. The removal of dams has become a politically contentious topic.*

involved where it shouldn't. But Chouinard wasn't deterred. "I just hope it gets around to a lot of people and changes their way of thinking about dams," he said. "I'd like to see a few more dams come down in my lifetime."[11]

POLITICAL STANCES

Throughout its time in business, Patagonia has never been shy about taking a hard line on an issue it believes in, even when it comes to politics. In the weeks and months leading up to national elections, Patagonia has teamed up with the nonpartisan voting advocacy group BallotReady to encourage people to make their voice heard and get out and vote. Patagonia closed its headquarters, distribution center, and stores nationwide on Election Day starting in 2016. It also created a section of its website that was solely dedicated to the election. The site gave consumers an option to enter their address in a search box to find a polling place, make a voting plan, and get information on requesting a ballot. The 2020 version posted a particularly direct message: "We need to elect climate leaders," it read. "The 2020 US Senate races will have a significant, long-lasting impact on the strength of our nation's climate policies and the existence of our wild places."[12]

The company didn't stop there. In September 2020, it was so fed up with what it viewed as the Trump Administration's disappointing stance on climate change that it produced its famous Regenerative Organic Stand Up shorts with a label that read: "Vote the a— out." The stunt went viral on Twitter. Company spokespeople were unapologetic. "We have been standing up to climate deniers for almost as long as we've been making those shorts," Corley Kenna, a Patagonia representative, told CNN Business.[13]

Much of the success of the company's outspoken activism dates to the hiring of Rose Marcario as chief financial officer in 2008. In 2014, Marcario was named Patagonia's chief

A LITTLE PUBLICITY STUNT

Many advertising campaigns at Patagonia take a long time to plan. But the idea behind the "Vote the a— out" campaign was hatched on a whim. It happened after Chouinard included the phrase at the end of a letter to the 1% for the Planet community in 2020. Someone from the design team saw it, and the team decided to include it on the shorts label. When Chouinard heard of the plan, his response was swift: "These are great. I need them in a size 32."

The stunt was a huge success, especially because Patagonia didn't tell the public in advance, instead letting consumers find the tags on their own. "The majority of Americans do think the climate crisis is real, and they do think we should be doing something about it," says Corley Kenna, Patagonia's director of global communications and public relations. "And so, when we say, 'Vote the a— out,' that's who we're referring to, is politicians from both parties who deny that climate change is real."[14]

executive officer. Since that time, the company has quadrupled its revenues and profits, started Tin Shed Ventures, and given away more than $90 million to environmental causes.[15]

"Patagonia has established a unique role in the political and policy ecosystem, and [they] are willing to be very public about their advocacy," said Neil Kornze, who was a director of the Bureau of Land Management under President Barack Obama and later ran an environmental consulting firm. "They are a group of avid environmentalists who just happen to sell coats."[16]

> *Patagonia's outspoken political approach was especially visible under chief executive officer Rose Marcario.*

CHAPTER EIGHT

"SAVE OUR HOME PLANET"

Patagonia continues to strive to be the environmentally, socially, and ethically responsible company it started out as. In the 2010s and 2020s, it upped its game by producing more and more products that push boundaries in terms of performance and endurance. As usual, the lineup included many firsts.

In 2018, the brand released its first-ever sleeping bag. The 850 Down Bag was inspired by a sleeping bag Chouinard had made for himself 45 years prior. The new ultra-lightweight bag was Fair Trade Certified and had a water-repellent finish. The goose-down filling was certified by NSF International to ensure

> *Today's Patagonia offers a wider assortment of products for outdoor enthusiasts than ever before.*

that the birds that supply the feathers are not force-fed or live-plucked.

In 2019, Patagonia recycled ten million plastic bottles to create its Black Hole Bag line of products. The body and webbing on these water-repellent bags were made of 100 percent recycled materials.[1] They were water resistant and Fair Trade Certified, and they featured the Bluesign label, a designation used to signify the product is safe for the environment and customers. The line included duffel bags, organizer cubes, packs, and totes.

That same year, Patagonia initiated its first partnership with another apparel company. It collaborated with footwear brand Danner to make the Foot Tractor Wading Boot. The shoe was designed for fly-fishing in wet conditions. A major fly-fishing website noted, "These are

BLUESIGN LABELS

Making clothing and keeping track of all the dyes, types of fabric, and methods used to create each garment is a time-consuming job. That's why Patagonia partnered with Bluesign Technologies, a company based in Switzerland. Bluesign's oversight ensures every step of the manufacturing process is safe for the environment, workers, and consumers. In 2007, Patagonia became the first brand to officially partner with Bluesign. For its 2021 spring line, nine out of Patagonia's top ten material suppliers were also Bluesign partners. Patagonia's actions have inspired other brands, manufacturers, and chemical suppliers to sign on with Bluesign too.

the best boots Patagonia has ever made and are designed to be the last boots you'll ever need to buy."[2]

FUN WITH FOOD

Patagonia is no longer just an outdoor clothing and gear company. It has also expanded into sourcing and selling food, and that business is growing. What began as an experiment in 2012 to produce sustainable wild salmon jerky has expanded into a full-fledged venture that sells everything from wine and sake to oil and vinegar to soup and chili to baby food.

Chouinard launched Patagonia Provisions to take a different path than conventional agriculture methods that use toxic pesticides and herbicides, waste water, and rely on synthetic fertilizer to grow. This impacts the topsoil. According to the United Nations Food and Agriculture Organization,

A REVOLUTIONARY GRAIN

In 2016, Patagonia teamed up with Hopworks Urban Brewery in Portland, Oregon, to produce a new drink called Long Root Ale. It was the first time anyone in the country had produced a beer made out of Kernza, a cousin of wheat. Kernza is unique for a few reasons. It has a large root system and grows quickly without the use of toxic pesticides. It uses less water to grow than wheat does. It also draws down more carbon from the atmosphere than other grains do. This is because when Kernza is harvested, its roots remain in the soil. The roots keep the carbon underground as they break down year after year.

91

> Patagonia Provisions sources its Wild Pink Salmon from self-sustaining runs in Washington state's Frasier River system.

if farmers around the world continue to degrade the soil by using conventional methods, the world will have only about 60 harvests left.[3]

Instead, Chouinard and Patagonia Provisions support regenerative organic farming practices. "With Provisions, we make that turn and step toward a new kind of future. One filled with deeply flavorful, nutritious foods that restore, rather than deplete, our planet. A future with widespread adoption of Regenerative Organic Certification, which ensures that food is produced in ways that build soil health, ensure animal welfare and protect agricultural workers," Chouinard says. "That's the revolution I want to be a part of."[4]

PATAGONIA ACTION WORKS

Heading into its fifth decade in business, Patagonia is still one of the top leaders in environmental advocacy and promoters of sustainable living around the world. In 2018, executives added a phrase to the company's mission statement to reflect its values: "We're in business to save our home planet." That same year, the company also launched a groundbreaking digital platform called Patagonia Action Works, which aimed to help people connect with nonprofit environmental organizations and

93

get more involved through outreach, in-person events, ballot initiatives, donations, and volunteer work. "If we could connect our community, friends and customers directly with local groups working on issues they are passionate about, suddenly these organizations would have the capacity to achieve even more. Everybody has a role to play in this movement," says Lisa Pike Sheehy, Patagonia's vice president of environment activism.[5]

A LAUNCH TO REMEMBER

In February 2018, Patagonia held an in-person event in Santa Monica, California, to launch Action Works, its new activism platform. As part of the festivities, company representatives curated a panel of activists of all ages who discussed their goals and hopes for the future. One panelist was Maricela Rosales, Latino Outdoors' Los Angeles coordinator. She talked about her work connecting Latino families and children to their surrounding environment. She also discussed her ongoing efforts to integrate racial justice and climate activism in her day-to-day life.

Users of the Action Works site can connect with more than 1,000 groups.[6] They can find potential partners by sorting by location or issue, such as land, water, climate, communities, and biodiversity. Participating organizations can set up a profile, search for member users, and recruit them to contribute a certain skill set, such as volunteer coordination, content development, or graphic design. Patagonia also holds in-person events at its retail stores to get the word out about the initiative and get people involved.

In the first six months of the program, more than 121,000 "meaningful advocacy actions" occurred, such as volunteering, donating funds, attending events, or signing petitions. The program generated more than $1.9 million in value for partner organizations. By February 2021, there had been more than 350,000 user sessions on the website.[7]

LOOKING TOWARD THE FUTURE

According to market research firm the NDP Group, Patagonia holds the top spot in the $12 billion outdoor apparel market.[8] Over its nearly 50 years in business, the outdoor brand has evolved into a leading presence in the retail space and one of the most outspoken supporters of sustainable business practices. It has accomplished many milestones. Nearly two-thirds of its products are made out of recycled materials. The outfitter has also donated millions in cash and in-kind donations to domestic and international grassroots environmental groups.

Patagonia has also become a leader in energy conservation and waste reduction. Starting in 2020, it used 100 percent renewable electricity in the United States and

WATER WASTE

Patagonia is taking strides to reduce its carbon footprint by making incremental but sweeping changes to its processes in all areas of its business. One area in which it is taking action is water conservation. First, it captures heating, ventilation, and air-conditioning condensation in buckets. Then it uses that moisture to water plants in its offices. The offices are equipped with low-flow toilets, showers, and faucets to conserve water. Patagonia headquarters also has an on-site bioswale. This is a series of culverts and natural areas that capture the rain and stormwater runoff from the roofs and parking lots. These areas have soil on top of gravel layers that allow stormwater to soak into the soil, which naturally filters it. The filtered water then feeds nearby plants or flows into the Ventura River, which flows into the ocean.

76 percent globally through on- and off-site solar panel installations. It has funded the installation of more than 1,000 solar panel systems on residential homes across the United States.[9] The company worked to install composting systems at all of its office, retail, and distribution locations. It was also doing away with single-use plastics in its café and stores.

But in spite of these notable steps, spokespeople from the brand say it has much further to go. In 2020, executives assessed where they wanted the company to be over the next decade. First, they hoped to use 100 percent renewable electricity in the company's

> *Patagonia's environmental initiatives are aimed at protecting the health and beauty of the natural environment.*

> *Many decades after founding the company, Chouinard remains passionate about Patagonia's mission and its place in the outdoor apparel industry.*

globally owned and operated facilities. Second, they put a plan in motion to become a zero-waste-to-landfill company by the end of 2025. That means all the company's waste products would go to recycling or compost, rather than the landfill. "We're committed to cleaning up our own act and have already begun to make the changes necessary so that by 2025 we will eliminate, capture or otherwise offset all of the carbon emissions we create," says Chouinard. "This includes not just our offices or stores, but all of the emissions from the factories that make our textiles and finished clothing and farms that grow our natural fibers. Eventually, we want to remove more carbon from the air than we put out."[10]

Chouinard is proud of the company he built out of a tin shed in his backyard. Even past the age of 80, he is as fired up as ever about the company's mission. "I've been asking myself why I still come into work. And it's not to sell more clothes or to make more money. It's because we're destroying the planet, and it's gotten so dire that we have to do something," he says. "What I really want to get across is that we're in an all-hands-on-deck type of situation. What's at stake is not only the future of some endangered species or large mammals; it's the future of humankind. And it's gonna happen within people's lifetimes. It's a whole different scenario now. So let's get on it."[11]

ESSENTIAL FACTS

KEY EVENTS

- In 1957, Yvon Chouinard buys himself a forge, anvil, and other tools and constructs his first rock climbing piton in his backyard.

- In 1965, Chouinard and his climbing buddy, aeronautical engineer Tom Frost, found Chouinard Equipment, a company that makes and sells equipment to climbers.

- In 1973, Chouinard Equipment breaks off to form a new company called Patagonia, which sells outdoor clothing such as rugby shirts, wool mittens, and rain jackets.

- In 1983, Patagonia becomes one of the first companies in the United States to provide on-site childcare for employees.

- In 1985, Patagonia announces that a portion of the company's revenue will be donated to environmental groups.

- In 2013, Patagonia sets up the program that will later be named Tin Shed Ventures, which is meant to help fund start-ups with an environmental focus.

- In 2017, Patagonia launches its Worn Wear website, an online version of the brand's program that allows consumers to turn in old products for repair, reuse, or recycling.

KEY PEOPLE

- Yvon Chouinard is an avid climber and outdoor enthusiast who cofounded Chouinard Equipment and, later, Patagonia.

- Malinda Chouinard is Yvon's wife, his longtime business partner, and co-owner of Patagonia.

- Tom Frost was Chouinard's climbing friend and an aeronautical engineer who helped him cofound Chouinard Equipment and later launch Patagonia as a brand.

- Rose Marcario was hired as Patagonia's chief financial officer in 2008 and promoted to chief executive officer in 2014.

- Doug Freeman, Patagonia's chief operating officer, works with the sales, marketing, and product teams to ensure the company's supply chain is running smoothly.

KEY PRODUCTS

- Straight Fit jeans: Made out of an organic cotton blend, these straight-leg jeans are unique because they are dyed with a process that uses less energy and water than conventional jeans-making processes.

- The Sender: The first garment of clothing that Chouinard Equipment sold, this striped, heavyweight cotton polo shirt became a staple for both climbing and everyday wear.

- The Snap-T pullover: This cozy pullover with two kangaroo pockets is made out of Synchilla fleece, a fuzzy, non-pilling fabric that wicks away moisture and started the fleece trend in outdoor gear.

- The Organic Cotton Snap-T pullover: Not just a simple remake of the Snap-T pullover, this heritage-inspired cozy sweatshirt broke the mold in the outdoor industry because it was the first to be made out of 100 percent organic cotton, avoiding the use of toxic pesticides and herbicides.

QUOTE

"At Patagonia, we appreciate that all life on earth is under threat of extinction. We aim to use the resources we have—our business, our investments, our voice and our imaginations—to do something about it."

—From Patagonia's mission statement

GLOSSARY

audit
An official inspection of a group or business's financial and organizational accounts, usually by an independent party.

bivouac sack
A temporary shelter, usually made out of weatherproof nylon or other durable fabric, that can house an individual for sleeping or camping.

burgeoning
Growing or expanding.

carabiner
A D-shaped clip usually made out of steel or aluminum and used to secure rope when climbing, caving, or sailing.

emblematic
Symbolic of something.

entrepreneurial
Business-savvy or capable of building a group or company from the ground up.

ethos
The overarching philosophy or spirit of something, such as a culture or group.

exploitation

The act of taking advantage of or treating people unfairly in order to benefit from their work.

grassroots

Something that is built from the ground up, as in community organizing.

hydrophilic

Having an ability to mix well with or blend in with water.

pilling

The formation of small balls or fuzz on the surface of a sweater or other clothing item after repeated wear.

piton

A metal spike that is driven into rocks and acts as an anchor for climbers.

rappelling

Lowering oneself down a mountain or rock face with the aid of a harness and climbing rope.

stewardship

The care of someone or something for positive gain.

sustainable

Meeting current needs without harming the ability of future generations to meet their needs.

ADDITIONAL RESOURCES

SELECTED BIBLIOGRAPHY

Chouinard, Yvon, and Vincent Stanley. *The Responsible Company: What We've Learned from Patagonia's First 40 Years.* Patagonia Books, 2012.

Paumgarten, Nick. "Patagonia's Philosopher-King." *New Yorker*, 16 Sept. 2016, newyorker.com. Accessed 8 Dec. 2021.

Sirtori-Cortina, Daniela. "From Climber to Billionaire: How Yvon Chouinard Built Patagonia into a Powerhouse His Own Way." *Forbes*, 20 May 2017, forbes.com. Accessed 5 Dec. 2021.

FURTHER READINGS

Nardo, Don. *Planet Under Siege: Climate Change.* ReferencePoint, 2020.

Roggio, Sarah. *Under Armour.* Abdo, 2023.

Yogerst, Joe. *100 Parks, 5,000 Ideas: Where to Go, When to Go, What to See, What to Do.* National Geographic, 2019.

ONLINE RESOURCES

To learn more about Patagonia, please visit **abdobooklinks.com** or scan this QR code. These links are routinely monitored and updated to provide the most current information available.

MORE INFORMATION

For more information on this subject, contact or visit the following organizations:

PATAGONIA HEADQUARTERS

235 W. Santa Clarita St.
Ventura, CA 93001
805-643-6074
patagonia.com/home

More than 1,500 people work at the Patagonia headquarters in sunny California. Patagonia was ranked one of the top 100 companies to work for in the United States by *Fortune* magazine in 2019.

YOSEMITE CLIMBING MUSEUM

5180 Highway 140
Mariposa, CA 95338
209-742-1000
yosemiteclimbingmuseum.com

This museum, built by the Yosemite Climbing Association, presents a fascinating history of rock climbing in the California region. It mostly focuses on the pioneers who built the climbing culture at Yosemite, including Patagonia founder Yvon Chouinard.

YOSEMITE NATIONAL PARK
PUBLIC INFORMATION OFFICE

PO Box 577
Yosemite, CA 95389
209-372-0200
nps.gov/yose/index.htm

Visitors to Yosemite National Park can learn about one of Yvon Chouinard's favorite places to rock climb in the United States. People can climb, hike, camp, kayak, and more throughout Yosemite's 1,200 square miles (3,100 sq km).

SOURCE NOTES

CHAPTER 1. AN ENVIRONMENTALLY AWARE BRAND

1. Rachel G. Clark. "Unfinished Business." *Patagonia*, n.d., patagonia.com. Accessed 3 Mar. 2022.

2. Clark, "Unfinished Business."

3. Clark, "Unfinished Business."

4. "Advanced Denim." *Patagonia*, n.d., patagonia.com. Accessed 3 Mar. 2022.

5. Clark, "Unfinished Business."

6. Clark, "Unfinished Business."

7. "Patagonia." *Craft*, n.d., craft.co. Accessed 3 Mar. 2022.

8. "Owned and Operated." *Patagonia*, n.d., patagonia.com. Accessed 3 Mar. 2022.

9. "Our Footprint." *Patagonia*, n.d., patagonia.com. Accessed 3 Mar. 2022.

10. "Patagonia's Mission Statement." *Patagonia*, n.d., patagonia.com. Accessed 3 Mar. 2022.

CHAPTER 2. A NATURALIST'S BEGINNING

1. Jian DeLeon. "What Patagonia Teaches Us About Building a Brand That Lasts." *Highsnobiety*, 2019, highsnobiety.com. Accessed 3 Mar. 2022.

2. "Company History." *Patagonia*, n.d., patagonia.com. Accessed 3 Mar. 2022.

3. "Company History."

4. DeLeon, "What Patagonia Teaches Us."

5. Daniel E. Slotnik. "Tom Frost, Mountaineer Who Designed a Cleaner Climb, Dies at 82." *New York Times*, 12 Sept. 2018, nytimes.com. Accessed 3 Mar. 2022.

6. DeLeon, "What Patagonia Teaches Us."

7. "The 1972 Chouinard Catalog." *Mountains and Minds*, n.d., mountainsandminds.org. Accessed 3 Mar. 2022.

8. "Patagonia – Men's Sender Rugby Shirt." *Countryside Ski & Climb*, n.d., countryside.co.uk. Accessed 3 Mar. 2022.

CHAPTER 3. THE BIRTH OF PATAGONIA

1. David Ebner. "How the Founder of Clothier Patagonia Became an Opponent of Dams." *Globe and Mail*, 19 Dec. 2014, theglobeandmail.com. Accessed 3 Mar. 2022.

2. Nick Paumgarten. "Patagonia's Philosopher-King." *New Yorker*, 12 Sept. 2016, newyorker.com. Accessed 3 Mar. 2022.

3. "Remembering Tom Frost." *Patagonia*, n.d., patagonia.com. Accessed 3 Mar. 2022.

4. David Gelles. "Patagonia's Deep-Rooted Activist Streak Fuels Suit against Trump." *Seattle Times*, 13 May 2018, seattletimes.com. Accessed 3 Mar. 2022.

CHAPTER 4. A CLOTHING REVOLUTION

1. Daniela Sirtori-Cortina. "From Climber to Billionaire: How Yvon Chouinard Built Patagonia into a Powerhouse His Own Way." *Forbes*, 20 Mar. 2017, forbes.com. Accessed 3 Mar. 2022.

2. Sirtori-Cortina, "From Climber to Billionaire."

3. David Ebner. "How the Founder of Clothier Patagonia Became an Opponent of Dams." *Globe and Mail*, 19 Dec. 2014, theglobeandmail.com. Accessed 3 Mar. 2022.

4. Brenden Gallagher. "'Uncommon Clothes for Uncommon People': A Brief History of Patagonia." *Grailed*, 1 Dec. 2017, grailed.com. Accessed 3 Mar. 2022.

5. "Company History." *Patagonia*, n.d., patagonia.com. Accessed 3 Mar. 2022.

6. Jian DeLeon. "What Patagonia Teaches Us About Building a Brand That Lasts." *Highsnobiety*, 2019, highsnobiety.com. Accessed 3 Mar. 2022.

7. Hilary Greenbaum and Dana Rubinstein. "The Evolution of Fleece, from Scratchy to Snuggie." *New York Times Magazine*, 25 Nov. 2011, nytimes.com. Accessed 3 Mar. 2022.

CHAPTER 5. PATAGONIA: AT THE OFFICE

1. Alex Rakestraw. "Around the World in Techwear: Every Outdoor Brand You Need to Know." *Highsnobiety*, n.d., highsnobiety.com. Accessed 3 Mar. 2022.

2. Adrianne Goodman. "Patagonia Lays Off 81 Employees in Ventura." *Los Angeles Times*, 3 July 1991, latimes.com. Accessed 3 Mar. 2022.

3. "Yvon Chouinard: Founding Patagonia and Living Simply." *Climate One*, 27 Oct. 2016, climateone.org. Accessed 3 Mar. 2022.

4. Goodman, "Patagonia Lays Off 81 Employees in Ventura."

5. Nick Paumgarten. "Patagonia's Philosopher-King." *New Yorker*, 12 Sept. 2016, newyorker.com. Accessed 3 Mar. 2022.

6. Paumgarten, "Patagonia's Philosopher-King."

7. Paumgarten, "Patagonia's Philosopher-King."

8. "Yvon Chouinard: Founding Patagonia and Living Simply."

9. "100 Best Companies to Work for: Patagonia." *Fortune*, n.d., fortune.com. Accessed 3 Mar. 2022.

10. "1% for the Planet." *Patagonia*, n.d., patagonia.com. Accessed 3 Mar. 2022.

11. "Who We Are." *The Conservation Alliance*, n.d., conservationalliance.com. Accessed 3 Mar. 2022.

12. "1% for the Planet."

13. Daniela Sirtori-Cortina. "From Climber to Billionaire: How Yvon Chouinard Built Patagonia into a Powerhouse His Own Way." *Forbes*, 20 Mar. 2017, forbes.com. Accessed 3 Mar. 2022.

14. "History." *Fair Labor Association*, 2012, fairlabor.org. Accessed 3 Mar. 2022.

SOURCE NOTES CONTINUED

CHAPTER 6. THE DO-GOOD COMPANY

1. Michele Bianchi. "How We Got Here: Organic Cotton." *Patagonia*, n.d., patagonia.com. Accessed 3 Mar. 2022.

2. Bianchi, "How We Got Here: Organic Cotton."

3. Lisa Polley. "Introducing the New Footprint Chronicles on Patagonia.com." *Patagonia*, n.d., patagonia.com. Accessed 3 Mar. 2022.

4. Katherine Martinko. "Patagonia Launches Worn Wear, an Online Store for Used Gear." *Treehugger*, 11 Oct. 2018, treehugger.com. Accessed 3 Mar. 2022.

5. Oliver Balch. "Patagonia Founder Yvon Chouinard: 'Denying Climate Change Is Evil.'" *Guardian*, 10 May 2019, theguardian.com. Accessed 3 Mar. 2022.

6. "Fair Trade." *Patagonia*, n.d., patagonia.com. Accessed 3 Mar. 2022.

7. "Tin Shed Ventures: Funding the Next Generation of Responsible Businesses." *Patagonia*, n.d., patagonia.com. Accessed 3 Mar. 2022.

8. "About." *Tin Shed Ventures*, n.d., tinshedventures.com. Accessed 3 Mar. 2022.

9. "Stories That Inspire." *Patagonia*, n.d., patagonia.com. Accessed 3 Mar. 2022.

10. Judith Rosen. "Patagonia's Book Program on Steady Climb." *Publishers Weekly*, 26 June 2015, publishersweekly.com. Accessed 3 Mar. 2022.

CHAPTER 7. BRAND CONTROVERSIES

1. "Global Estimates of Modern Slavery." *International Labor Organization*, n.d., ilo.org. Accessed 3 Mar. 2022.

2. Gillian B. White. "All Your Clothes Are Made with Exploited Labor." *Atlantic*, 3 June 2015, theatlantic.com. Accessed 3 Mar. 2022.

3. White, "All Your Clothes Are Made with Exploited Labor."

4. White, "All Your Clothes Are Made with Exploited Labor."

5. "Activism." *Patagonia*, n.d., patagonia.com.au. Accessed 3 Mar. 2022.

6. Simonetta Lein. "Why Sustainable Branding Matters." *Forbes*, 20 Aug. 2018, forbes.com. Accessed 3 Mar. 2022.

7. David Gelles. "Patagonia v. Trump." *New York Times*, 5 May 2018, nytimes.com. Accessed 3 Mar. 2022.

8. Gelles, "Patagonia v. Trump."

9. Katie Klingsporn. "Behind the Scenes Filming 'DamNation.'" *Patagonia*, n.d., patagonia.com. Accessed 3 Mar. 2022.

10. Jeff Beer. "What Patagonia Learned from Mixing Content Strategy and Activism." *Fast Company*, 20 Oct. 2015, fastcompany.com. Accessed 3 Mar. 2022.

11. Klingsporn, "Behind the Scenes Filming 'DamNation.'"

12. Alexis Benveniste. "New Patagonia Tags: 'Vote the A— Out.'" *CNN Business*, 15 Sept. 2020, cnn.com. Accessed 3 Mar. 2022.

13. Benveniste, "New Patagonia Tags."

14. Jonathan Evans. "The Full Story Behind Patagonia's 'Vote the A— Out' Tags." *Esquire*, 19 Sept. 2020, esquire.com. Accessed 3 Mar. 2022.

15. Gelles, "Patagonia v. Trump."

16. Gelles, "Patagonia v. Trump."

CHAPTER 8. "SAVE OUR HOME PLANET"

1. "Bluesign System." *Patagonia*, n.d., patagonia.com. Accessed 3 Mar. 2022.

2. "Patagonia x Danner Foot Tractor Wading Boots." *Fly Fishers Fly Shop*, n.d., theflyfishers.com. Accessed 3 Mar. 2022.

3. Yvon Chouinard. "Why Food?" *Patagonia Provisions*, 23 Apr. 2020, patagoniaprovisions.com. Accessed 3 Mar. 2022.

4. Chouinard, "Why Food?"

5. Jack Stanley. "Patagonia to Launch Environmental Activism Platform." *Hypebeast*, 7 Feb. 2018, hypebeast.com. Accessed 3 Mar. 2022.

6. "Patagonia Action Works." *Shorty Awards*, n.d., shortyawards.com. Accessed 3 Mar. 2022.

7. "Patagonia Action Works."

8. Maggie Overfelt. "As The North Face Battles Patagonia in Outdoors Market, It Bets Tackling Climate Change Will Pay Off." *CNBC*, 14 Aug. 2020, cnbc.com. Accessed 3 Mar. 2022.

9. "Owned and Operated." *Patagonia*, n.d., patagonia.com. Accessed 3 Mar. 2022.

10. Brad Wieners. "What's at Stake Is the Future of Humankind." *Patagonia*, n.d., patagonia.com. Accessed 3 Mar. 2022.

11. Wieners, "What's at Stake."

INDEX

Advanced Denim method, 11
American Apparel, 40
apparel colors, 10–11, 26, 41, 44, 65

Baggies, 45
Barbour, Helen, 12
Bears Ears National Monument, 79
benefit corporation status, 70–71
Black Diamond Equipment, 30
Bluesign Technologies, 90
Bondurant, Rob, 48
boots, 90–91
Boston, Massachusetts, 63
boycotts, 80

Capelli, Mark, 34–35, 36
Capilene polyester, 46
carbon emissions, 9–10, 11, 65, 91, 96, 98–99
childcare, 53–54, 56
chocks, 24, 27
Chouinard, Malinda, 30, 33, 34, 53, 54
Chouinard, Yvon, 17–27, 29–31, 33–35, 39–40, 45–46, 48, 51–54, 56, 60, 69–71, 73, 81, 84, 85, 89, 91–93, 98–99
Chouinard Equipment, 21, 22, 24, 26–27, 29, 30, 35, 71
climbing, 5, 18, 20–27, 29–34, 35, 39, 44, 46, 47, 56, 57
Clinton, Bill, 60, 61

clothing repair, 6, 12, 67
commercials, 34, 79
company culture, 14, 53–56
company name, 30, 31
Conservation Alliance, 57
cotton, 7, 11, 26, 32, 33, 41, 64, 65

DamNation, 83
dams, 35, 57, 81–84
Denny, Glen, 73
"Don't Buy This Jacket," 67–68

elections, 84
employee benefits, 56
environmental campaigns, 34–36, 64, 69–70
Environmental Protection Agency, 66

Fair Labor Association, 60
Fair Trade Certified, 9, 14, 70, 75, 89–90
falconry, 18, 29
fast fashion, 41, 67
films, 31, 83
Fitz Roy, 31
Footprint Chronicles, 66
Freeman, Doug, 77
Friends of the Ventura River, 35, 36
Frost, Tom, 20–24, 30, 33, 35

jeans, 5–12

110

Kenna, Corley, 85
Kernza, 91
Kornze, Neil, 87

labor trafficking, 76, 77
layering, 12, 33, 41, 42–43, 46, 65
Let My People Go Surfing, 17, 71–73
Little, Mark, 5–7, 8, 10
logo, 30–31, 51

mafia, 52
Marcario, Rose, 85
mission statement, 14–15, 93

No Sweat Initiative, 61

Obama, Barack, 53, 87
Olsen, Karla, 73
1% for the Planet, 57, 73, 85
Organic Cotton Snap-T pullover, 65
outdoor apparel industry, 95

Patagonia Action Works, 93–95
Patagonia Books, 73
Patagonia Common Threads
   Initiative, 67
Patagonia Provisions, 91–93
pile fleece jacket, 32
pitons, 20–23, 24, 27
polypropylene, 41, 42, 46
product guarantee, 12
product testing, 11, 45–46

Quality Assurance (QA) team, 59

recycled materials, 11, 14, 47, 48, 60,
   65, 67, 90, 95, 98
Regenerative Organic cotton, 11, 65
renewable energy, 14, 71, 95–96
Responsible Company, The, 73
Rosales, Maricela, 94

Sender rugby shirt, 26
sleeping bags, 12, 89
Snap-T pullover, 47, 48–49, 65
Stand Up shorts, 31–32, 45, 85
Storm jacket, 47, 49
supply chain, 57, 61, 64, 66, 76–77
Sweeney, Kevin, 52
Synchilla fleece, 47, 48

Tin Shed Ventures, 71, 87
Tools for Grassroots Activists, 73
Trump, Donald, 79, 85

Ventura, California, 22, 30, 52, 54
Ventura River, 34–35, 36, 96

water conservation, 71, 96
Worn Wear, 67–68

Yosemite, 20–21, 35, 70, 73

ABOUT THE AUTHOR

ALEXIS BURLING

Alexis Burling has written dozens of articles and books for young readers on a variety of topics ranging from current events and biographies of famous people to nutrition and fitness, careers, and money management. She is also a professional book critic with reviews of adult and young adult books, author interviews, and other publishing industry–related articles published in the *New York Times*, the *Washington Post Book World*, the *San Francisco Chronicle*, and more. Burling wears Patagonia gear whenever she's backpacking throughout the Pacific Northwest. She lives in White Salmon, Washington, with her husband and their cat, Suki.

ABOUT THE CONSULTANT

HUIJU PARK

Huiju Park (PhD) is an associate professor of Apparel Design in the Department of Human Centered Design at Cornell University (Ithaca, New York). Professor Park obtained his PhD at Oklahoma State University with an expertise in functional apparel design after working at Puma Korea for five years as a team sports product line manager and footwear merchandiser. Since Professor Park joined Cornell University in 2011, he has participated in multiple funded multidisciplinary research projects aiming to improve sports apparel, ballistic body armor, chemical and biological protective clothing, and firefighters' bunker gear. Professor Park has taught Activewear Design and Product Development, Fashion CAD, Functional Aspects of Clothing and Design, and Smart Clothing Design and Programming at Cornell University.